50 Time Saving Dishes to Cook at Home

By: Kelly Johnson

Table of Contents

- Spaghetti Aglio e Olio
- Stir-Fried Rice
- Grilled Cheese Sandwich
- Chicken Caesar Salad
- Tacos
- Veggie Quesadilla
- One-Pan Baked Salmon
- Chicken Stir-Fry
- Sheet Pan Chicken and Veggies
- Avocado Toast
- Omelette
- Fried Rice with Leftover Veggies
- Tuna Salad
- Instant Pot Chili
- Egg Fried Rice
- Pita Pockets with Hummus and Veggies
- Baked Ziti

- Instant Pot Pasta
- Grilled Shrimp Skewers
- Smoothie Bowl
- Caprese Salad
- Chicken Wraps
- Baked Sweet Potatoes
- Roasted Veggie Salad
- Grilled Chicken Salad
- Pasta with Marinara Sauce
- Quick Stir-Fry Noodles
- Shrimp Tacos
- Chicken and Veggie Skewers
- Miso Soup
- Veggie Soup
- Rice Paper Rolls
- Scrambled Eggs with Spinach
- Breakfast Burrito
- BLT Sandwich
- Quick Baked Chicken Breasts

- Veggie Tacos
- Tomato Soup with Grilled Cheese
- Chicken Fajitas
- Pasta Primavera
- Instant Pot Risotto
- Burrito Bowl
- Quick Fried Egg Sandwich
- Ramen with Vegetables
- Chicken Pita Wraps
- Sautéed Shrimp with Garlic
- Stir-Fry Tofu
- Nachos
- Pita Pizza
- Simple Sautéed Vegetables

Gnocchi with Brown Butter Sage

Ingredients:

- 1 lb gnocchi
- 4 tbsp unsalted butter
- 10 fresh sage leaves
- 1/4 cup grated Parmesan cheese
- Salt and pepper, to taste

Instructions:

1. Cook gnocchi according to package instructions. Drain and set aside.
2. In a large pan, melt butter over medium heat. Once melted, add sage leaves and cook until butter turns golden brown and fragrant (about 3 minutes).
3. Add cooked gnocchi to the pan and toss to coat in the brown butter.
4. Season with salt and pepper, then serve topped with grated Parmesan.

Kimchi Noodles

Ingredients:

- 8 oz noodles (ramen or udon)
- 1/2 cup kimchi, chopped
- 1 tbsp vegetable oil
- 2 cloves garlic, minced
- 2 tbsp soy sauce
- 1 tbsp gochujang (Korean chili paste)
- 1 tbsp rice vinegar
- 1 tbsp sesame oil
- 1 tbsp sesame seeds
- 1/4 cup green onions, chopped

Instructions:

1. Cook noodles according to package instructions. Drain and set aside.
2. In a pan, heat vegetable oil over medium heat. Add garlic and sauté until fragrant.
3. Add chopped kimchi and cook for 2-3 minutes.
4. Stir in soy sauce, gochujang, rice vinegar, and sesame oil.
5. Toss in the cooked noodles and mix well.
6. Garnish with sesame seeds and green onions before serving.

Shoyu Ramen

Ingredients:

- 2 packs ramen noodles
- 4 cups chicken or pork broth
- 2 tbsp soy sauce
- 1 tbsp mirin
- 1 tbsp sesame oil
- 1 tsp ginger, grated
- 2 cloves garlic, minced
- 1/4 cup green onions, chopped
- 1/4 cup nori, shredded
- Soft-boiled egg (optional)

Instructions:

1. Cook ramen noodles according to package instructions. Drain and set aside.
2. In a pot, heat sesame oil over medium heat. Add garlic and ginger, sauté until fragrant.
3. Add the broth, soy sauce, and mirin to the pot. Bring to a simmer.
4. Divide cooked noodles into bowls and pour broth over the noodles.
5. Garnish with green onions, nori, and soft-boiled egg, if desired.

Garlic Butter Shrimp Pasta

Ingredients:

- 8 oz pasta (linguine or spaghetti)
- 1 lb shrimp, peeled and deveined
- 4 tbsp butter
- 6 cloves garlic, minced
- 1/2 cup white wine (optional)
- 1/4 cup Parmesan cheese, grated
- Salt and pepper, to taste
- 2 tbsp parsley, chopped

Instructions:

1. Cook pasta according to package instructions. Drain and set aside.
2. In a large skillet, melt butter over medium heat. Add garlic and sauté until fragrant.
3. Add shrimp to the pan and cook until pink, about 3-4 minutes.
4. Add white wine (if using) and cook for another minute.
5. Toss in the cooked pasta and mix until the pasta is coated with the garlic butter.
6. Season with salt and pepper, and top with Parmesan and parsley before serving.

Chicken Noodle Soup

Ingredients:

- 2 tbsp olive oil
- 1 onion, chopped
- 2 carrots, sliced
- 2 celery stalks, chopped
- 2 cloves garlic, minced
- 6 cups chicken broth
- 1 lb chicken breast or thighs, cooked and shredded
- 1 1/2 cups egg noodles
- Salt and pepper, to taste
- 1/4 cup parsley, chopped

Instructions:

1. In a pot, heat olive oil over medium heat. Add onion, carrots, and celery. Cook until softened, about 5-7 minutes.
2. Add garlic and cook for 1 minute.
3. Pour in chicken broth and bring to a boil.
4. Add the shredded chicken and egg noodles. Cook for 10 minutes, until noodles are tender.
5. Season with salt and pepper, and garnish with parsley before serving.

Veggie Stir-Fry Noodles

Ingredients:

- 8 oz noodles (rice noodles or lo mein)
- 1 tbsp vegetable oil
- 1 bell pepper, sliced
- 1 carrot, julienned
- 1 zucchini, sliced
- 1/2 cup snap peas
- 2 tbsp soy sauce
- 1 tbsp hoisin sauce
- 1 tbsp sesame oil
- 1 tbsp sesame seeds
- Green onions, chopped

Instructions:

1. Cook noodles according to package instructions. Drain and set aside.
2. In a pan, heat vegetable oil over medium heat. Add bell pepper, carrot, zucchini, and snap peas. Stir-fry for 5-6 minutes.
3. Stir in soy sauce, hoisin sauce, and sesame oil.
4. Add cooked noodles and toss to combine.
5. Garnish with sesame seeds and green onions before serving.

Seafood Noodles

Ingredients:

- 8 oz noodles (egg noodles or spaghetti)
- 1 tbsp olive oil
- 1/2 lb shrimp, peeled and deveined
- 1/2 lb scallops
- 2 cloves garlic, minced
- 1/4 cup white wine
- 1/4 cup heavy cream
- 1/4 cup Parmesan cheese, grated
- Salt and pepper, to taste
- Fresh parsley, chopped

Instructions:

1. Cook noodles according to package instructions. Drain and set aside.
2. In a large skillet, heat olive oil over medium heat. Add garlic and sauté until fragrant.
3. Add shrimp and scallops to the pan and cook until golden and opaque, about 3-4 minutes per side.
4. Pour in white wine and let it reduce by half.
5. Add heavy cream and Parmesan cheese, stirring to combine.

6. Toss in the cooked noodles and coat with the sauce.

7. Season with salt and pepper, and garnish with fresh parsley before serving.

Carbonara Noodles

Ingredients:

- 8 oz pasta (spaghetti or fettuccine)
- 4 oz pancetta or bacon, diced
- 2 eggs
- 1/2 cup Parmesan cheese, grated
- Salt and pepper, to taste
- 1 tbsp parsley, chopped

Instructions:

1. Cook pasta according to package instructions. Drain, reserving 1/2 cup of pasta water.
2. In a pan, cook pancetta or bacon until crispy, about 5-6 minutes.
3. In a bowl, whisk eggs with Parmesan cheese, salt, and pepper.
4. Add cooked pasta to the pan with pancetta, and toss to combine.
5. Remove from heat and quickly pour the egg mixture over the pasta. Toss well to coat the noodles.
6. Add reserved pasta water to reach desired consistency.
7. Garnish with parsley and serve immediately.

Pad Woon Sen

Ingredients:

- 8 oz glass noodles
- 1 tbsp vegetable oil
- 2 cloves garlic, minced
- 1 egg, beaten
- 1/2 cup carrots, julienned
- 1/2 cup bell peppers, sliced
- 1/4 cup soy sauce
- 1 tbsp fish sauce
- 1 tbsp oyster sauce
- 1 tsp sugar
- 1/4 cup cilantro, chopped
- Lime wedges for serving

Instructions:

1. Cook glass noodles according to package instructions. Drain and set aside.
2. In a pan, heat vegetable oil over medium heat. Add garlic and sauté until fragrant.
3. Push garlic to one side and add the beaten egg to the pan. Scramble the egg until cooked.
4. Add carrots and bell peppers, cooking for 2-3 minutes.

5. Stir in soy sauce, fish sauce, oyster sauce, and sugar.

6. Add the cooked noodles and toss to coat.

7. Garnish with cilantro and serve with lime wedges.

Tonkotsu Ramen

Ingredients:

- 2 packs ramen noodles
- 4 cups pork broth
- 2 tbsp soy sauce
- 1 tbsp miso paste
- 1 tbsp sesame oil
- 1 tsp ginger, grated
- 2 cloves garlic, minced
- 2 eggs (soft-boiled)
- 1/4 cup green onions, chopped
- 1/4 cup nori, shredded

Instructions:

1. Cook ramen noodles according to package instructions. Drain and set aside.
2. In a pot, heat sesame oil over medium heat. Add garlic and ginger, sauté until fragrant.
3. Pour in pork broth, soy sauce, and miso paste. Simmer for 10-15 minutes.
4. Divide cooked noodles into bowls and pour broth over the noodles.
5. Garnish with soft-boiled eggs, green onions, and shredded nori.

Pho Ga

Ingredients:

- 1 lb chicken breast or thighs
- 1 onion, quartered
- 2-inch piece of ginger, sliced
- 2 cloves garlic, smashed
- 2 cinnamon sticks
- 4 star anise
- 4 cups chicken broth
- 1 tbsp fish sauce
- 8 oz rice noodles
- 1/4 cup cilantro, chopped
- 1/4 cup basil, chopped
- Lime wedges
- Bean sprouts

Instructions:

1. In a large pot, add chicken, onion, ginger, garlic, cinnamon sticks, and star anise.
2. Pour in chicken broth and bring to a boil.
3. Reduce heat and simmer for 30 minutes.

4. Remove chicken, shred it, and return it to the pot.

5. Add fish sauce and cook rice noodles according to package instructions.

6. Serve the pho with fresh cilantro, basil, lime wedges, and bean sprouts.

Spaghetti Aglio e Olio

Ingredients:

- 8 oz spaghetti
- 1/4 cup olive oil
- 4 cloves garlic, thinly sliced
- 1/2 tsp red pepper flakes
- Salt and pepper, to taste
- 1/4 cup chopped parsley
- Freshly grated Parmesan cheese (optional)

Instructions:

1. Cook spaghetti according to package instructions. Drain, reserving 1/2 cup of pasta water.
2. In a large pan, heat olive oil over medium heat. Add garlic and sauté until golden, about 1-2 minutes.
3. Add red pepper flakes and toss the cooked pasta into the pan. Stir to combine.
4. Add some reserved pasta water if needed to coat the pasta.
5. Season with salt and pepper, and garnish with chopped parsley. Top with Parmesan if desired.

Stir-Fried Rice

Ingredients:

- 2 cups cooked rice (preferably day-old)
- 2 tbsp vegetable oil
- 2 eggs, beaten
- 1 onion, chopped
- 1 cup mixed vegetables (carrots, peas, corn)
- 2 cloves garlic, minced
- 3 tbsp soy sauce
- 1 tbsp sesame oil
- Green onions, chopped for garnish

Instructions:

1. Heat 1 tbsp vegetable oil in a pan over medium heat. Scramble the eggs until cooked, then set them aside.
2. In the same pan, add another tablespoon of oil and sauté onion, garlic, and mixed vegetables for 5 minutes until softened.
3. Add rice and stir to break up clumps. Cook for 3-4 minutes, stirring occasionally.
4. Stir in soy sauce and sesame oil, and mix well.
5. Add cooked eggs and stir to combine.
6. Garnish with green onions and serve.

Grilled Cheese Sandwich

Ingredients:

- 2 slices of bread
- 2 tbsp butter
- 2 slices cheddar cheese (or any cheese of your choice)

Instructions:

1. Butter one side of each bread slice.
2. Heat a skillet over medium heat. Place one slice of bread, buttered side down, in the skillet.
3. Place cheese slices on top and cover with the second slice of bread, buttered side up.
4. Grill for 3-4 minutes on each side, until golden brown and the cheese is melted.
5. Remove from the skillet, slice, and serve.

Chicken Caesar Salad

Ingredients:

- 2 chicken breasts, grilled and sliced
- 4 cups Romaine lettuce, chopped
- 1/2 cup Caesar dressing
- 1/4 cup Parmesan cheese, grated
- Croutons, for garnish

Instructions:

1. Grill or cook chicken breasts, then slice them into thin strips.
2. Toss the lettuce with Caesar dressing until well-coated.
3. Top the salad with sliced chicken, grated Parmesan cheese, and croutons.
4. Serve immediately.

Tacos

Ingredients:

- 1 lb ground beef (or chicken, pork, or tofu)
- 1 packet taco seasoning (or homemade seasoning)
- 8 taco shells (hard or soft)
- Toppings: lettuce, diced tomatoes, cheese, sour cream, salsa, avocado

Instructions:

1. Cook ground beef in a skillet over medium heat, breaking it up as it cooks.
2. Stir in taco seasoning and a splash of water (as directed on the seasoning packet).
3. Cook until the meat is browned and fully cooked.
4. Warm taco shells according to package instructions.
5. Fill each taco shell with seasoned meat and top with your desired toppings.
6. Serve immediately.

Veggie Quesadilla

Ingredients:

- 2 flour tortillas
- 1 cup shredded cheese (cheddar or Mexican blend)
- 1/2 cup bell pepper, chopped
- 1/2 cup onion, chopped
- 1/2 cup mushrooms, sliced
- 1 tbsp olive oil

Instructions:

1. Heat olive oil in a pan over medium heat. Add bell pepper, onion, and mushrooms. Cook until softened, about 5 minutes.

2. Heat a separate pan over medium heat. Place one tortilla in the pan and sprinkle with half of the shredded cheese.

3. Add the cooked veggies on top, then sprinkle the remaining cheese.

4. Top with the second tortilla and cook for 2-3 minutes on each side until golden brown and the cheese is melted.

5. Remove from the pan, slice, and serve.

One-Pan Baked Salmon

Ingredients:

- 2 salmon fillets
- 2 tbsp olive oil
- 1 lemon, sliced
- 2 cloves garlic, minced
- Salt and pepper, to taste
- Fresh dill or parsley, for garnish

Instructions:

1. Preheat oven to 400°F (200°C).
2. Place salmon fillets on a baking sheet lined with parchment paper. Drizzle with olive oil and sprinkle with garlic, salt, and pepper.
3. Lay lemon slices on top of the salmon.
4. Bake for 12-15 minutes, until the salmon is cooked through and flakes easily with a fork.
5. Garnish with fresh dill or parsley and serve.

Chicken Stir-Fry

Ingredients:

- 2 chicken breasts, sliced into strips
- 2 tbsp soy sauce
- 1 tbsp oyster sauce
- 1 tbsp sesame oil
- 1 tbsp vegetable oil
- 1 bell pepper, sliced
- 1 carrot, julienned
- 1/2 cup snap peas
- 2 cloves garlic, minced
- 1/4 cup green onions, chopped

Instructions:

1. Heat vegetable oil in a large pan over medium heat. Add chicken and cook until browned and cooked through, about 5-7 minutes.
2. Add garlic, bell pepper, carrot, and snap peas to the pan and cook for another 5 minutes, stirring occasionally.
3. Stir in soy sauce, oyster sauce, and sesame oil.
4. Cook for an additional 2 minutes, then garnish with green onions.
5. Serve over rice or noodles.

Sheet Pan Chicken and Veggies

Ingredients:

- 4 bone-in, skin-on chicken thighs
- 1 cup baby potatoes, halved
- 1 cup carrots, chopped
- 1 cup broccoli florets
- 2 tbsp olive oil
- 1 tsp garlic powder
- 1 tsp paprika
- Salt and pepper, to taste

Instructions:

1. Preheat the oven to 400°F (200°C).
2. Arrange chicken thighs, potatoes, carrots, and broccoli on a sheet pan.
3. Drizzle with olive oil and sprinkle with garlic powder, paprika, salt, and pepper.
4. Toss everything to coat evenly.
5. Roast for 35-40 minutes, or until the chicken is cooked through and the vegetables are tender.
6. Serve immediately.

Avocado Toast

Ingredients:

- 2 slices of bread
- 1 ripe avocado
- Salt and pepper, to taste
- Red pepper flakes (optional)
- Olive oil (optional)
- Lemon juice (optional)

Instructions:

1. Toast the bread slices to your desired level of crispness.
2. While the bread is toasting, mash the avocado with a fork in a bowl.
3. Add salt, pepper, and a squeeze of lemon juice if desired.
4. Spread the mashed avocado onto the toasted bread.
5. Optionally drizzle with olive oil and sprinkle with red pepper flakes for extra flavor.
6. Serve immediately.

Omelette

Ingredients:

- 3 eggs
- 2 tbsp milk (optional)
- Salt and pepper, to taste
- 1/4 cup cheese, grated (optional)
- 1/4 cup vegetables (e.g., bell pepper, onion, spinach), chopped
- 1 tbsp butter or oil for cooking

Instructions:

1. Crack the eggs into a bowl and whisk with milk, salt, and pepper.
2. Heat butter or oil in a pan over medium heat.
3. Pour in the egg mixture and swirl the pan to evenly coat the bottom.
4. As the eggs start to set, sprinkle cheese and vegetables on one half.
5. Fold the omelette in half and cook for another 1-2 minutes until the eggs are fully set.
6. Slide onto a plate and serve.

Fried Rice with Leftover Veggies

Ingredients:

- 2 cups cooked rice (preferably day-old)
- 2 tbsp vegetable oil
- 1/2 cup mixed vegetables (carrots, peas, corn, etc.)
- 2 eggs, beaten
- 2 tbsp soy sauce
- 1/2 onion, chopped
- 2 cloves garlic, minced
- Green onions, chopped for garnish

Instructions:

1. Heat vegetable oil in a pan or wok over medium-high heat.
2. Add onions and garlic, sautéing until softened.
3. Add mixed vegetables and cook for 2-3 minutes.
4. Push the veggies to one side and scramble the beaten eggs on the other side.
5. Add the rice, breaking up any clumps. Stir in soy sauce and cook for 3-4 minutes until everything is heated through.
6. Garnish with green onions and serve.

Tuna Salad

Ingredients:

- 1 can tuna, drained
- 2 tbsp mayonnaise
- 1 tbsp Dijon mustard
- 1/4 cup celery, chopped
- 1/4 cup red onion, chopped
- Salt and pepper, to taste
- 1 tsp lemon juice (optional)

Instructions:

1. In a bowl, combine tuna, mayonnaise, Dijon mustard, celery, and red onion.
2. Mix well and season with salt, pepper, and lemon juice.
3. Serve on a bed of greens, in a sandwich, or in a pita pocket.

Instant Pot Chili

Ingredients:

- 1 lb ground beef or turkey
- 1 onion, chopped
- 2 cloves garlic, minced
- 1 can (15 oz) kidney beans, drained and rinsed
- 1 can (15 oz) black beans, drained and rinsed
- 1 can (15 oz) diced tomatoes
- 2 tbsp chili powder
- 1 tsp cumin
- 1 tsp smoked paprika
- 1/2 tsp salt
- 1/4 tsp black pepper
- 1 cup beef or vegetable broth

Instructions:

1. Set the Instant Pot to sauté mode and cook the ground meat with onions and garlic until browned.
2. Add the beans, tomatoes, chili powder, cumin, paprika, salt, and pepper.
3. Pour in the broth and stir to combine.
4. Close the lid and set to cook on high pressure for 10 minutes.
5. Quick release the pressure and stir before serving.

Egg Fried Rice

Ingredients:

- 2 cups cooked rice (preferably day-old)
- 2 tbsp vegetable oil
- 2 eggs, beaten
- 1/4 cup peas and carrots (frozen is fine)
- 2 tbsp soy sauce
- 1/2 onion, chopped
- 2 cloves garlic, minced
- Green onions, chopped for garnish

Instructions:

1. Heat vegetable oil in a large pan or wok over medium-high heat.
2. Add onions and garlic and sauté until softened.
3. Add peas and carrots and cook for 2-3 minutes.
4. Push veggies to the side of the pan and scramble the beaten eggs on the other side.
5. Add the rice and soy sauce, stir to combine, and cook for 3-4 minutes.
6. Garnish with green onions and serve.

Pita Pockets with Hummus and Veggies

Ingredients:

- 4 pita pockets
- 1 cup hummus
- 1 cucumber, sliced
- 1 tomato, sliced
- 1/4 red onion, sliced
- 1/2 cup spinach or lettuce
- Feta cheese (optional)

Instructions:

1. Cut the pita pockets in half to open them.
2. Spread a generous amount of hummus inside each pita half.
3. Stuff with cucumber, tomato, onion, and spinach.
4. Top with feta cheese if desired.
5. Serve immediately.

Baked Ziti

Ingredients:

- 1 lb ziti pasta
- 2 cups marinara sauce
- 1 lb ricotta cheese
- 2 cups mozzarella cheese, shredded
- 1/2 cup Parmesan cheese, grated
- Salt and pepper, to taste
- Fresh basil, chopped (optional)

Instructions:

1. Preheat oven to 375°F (190°C).
2. Cook ziti pasta according to package directions. Drain and set aside.
3. In a large mixing bowl, combine marinara sauce, ricotta, and half of the mozzarella cheese.
4. Add the cooked pasta and stir to combine.
5. Pour into a baking dish and top with remaining mozzarella and Parmesan cheese.
6. Bake for 20-25 minutes until the cheese is bubbly and golden.
7. Garnish with fresh basil and serve.

Instant Pot Pasta

Ingredients:

- 1 lb pasta
- 4 cups water or broth
- 1 jar (24 oz) marinara sauce
- 1/2 tsp garlic powder
- 1/2 tsp onion powder
- Salt and pepper, to taste
- Parmesan cheese, for garnish (optional)

Instructions:

1. Add pasta, water or broth, marinara sauce, garlic powder, onion powder, salt, and pepper to the Instant Pot.
2. Set to cook on high pressure for 4-6 minutes, depending on the pasta type.
3. Quick release the pressure and stir the pasta.
4. Garnish with Parmesan cheese and serve.

Grilled Shrimp Skewers

Ingredients:

- 1 lb shrimp, peeled and deveined
- 2 tbsp olive oil
- 2 cloves garlic, minced
- 1 tsp smoked paprika
- 1/2 tsp lemon zest
- Salt and pepper, to taste
- Lemon wedges for serving

Instructions:

1. In a bowl, combine olive oil, garlic, smoked paprika, lemon zest, salt, and pepper.
2. Toss shrimp in the marinade and let sit for 15-20 minutes.
3. Preheat the grill to medium-high heat.
4. Thread shrimp onto skewers and grill for 2-3 minutes per side until pink and cooked through.
5. Serve with lemon wedges.

Smoothie Bowl

Ingredients:

- 1 frozen banana
- 1/2 cup frozen berries (e.g., strawberries, blueberries)
- 1/2 cup almond milk or any milk of choice
- 1/4 cup Greek yogurt (optional for extra creaminess)
- Toppings: granola, chia seeds, fresh fruit, coconut flakes, honey

Instructions:

1. In a blender, combine the frozen banana, berries, almond milk, and Greek yogurt (if using).
2. Blend until smooth and thick.
3. Pour into a bowl and top with granola, chia seeds, fresh fruit, coconut flakes, and a drizzle of honey.
4. Serve immediately.

Caprese Salad

Ingredients:

- 2 cups fresh mozzarella, sliced
- 2 large tomatoes, sliced
- Fresh basil leaves
- Balsamic glaze
- Olive oil
- Salt and pepper, to taste

Instructions:

1. On a serving plate, alternate layers of sliced mozzarella, tomatoes, and fresh basil.
2. Drizzle with olive oil and balsamic glaze.
3. Season with salt and pepper.
4. Serve immediately as a refreshing side salad.

Chicken Wraps

Ingredients:

- 2 chicken breasts, cooked and sliced
- 4 large flour tortillas
- 1/2 cup lettuce, shredded
- 1/2 cup tomato, diced
- 1/4 cup shredded cheese (cheddar, mozzarella, or your choice)
- 1/4 cup ranch or Caesar dressing (optional)

Instructions:

1. Lay out the tortillas on a flat surface.
2. In the center of each tortilla, layer sliced chicken, lettuce, tomato, and cheese.
3. Drizzle with your choice of dressing.
4. Fold in the sides of the tortilla and roll up tightly.
5. Slice in half and serve.

Baked Sweet Potatoes

Ingredients:

- 4 medium sweet potatoes
- Olive oil
- Salt and pepper, to taste

Instructions:

1. Preheat the oven to 400°F (200°C).
2. Scrub the sweet potatoes and prick them a few times with a fork.
3. Rub with olive oil and season with salt and pepper.
4. Place on a baking sheet and bake for 40-45 minutes or until tender when pierced with a fork.
5. Serve as a side dish or topped with your favorite ingredients.

Roasted Veggie Salad

Ingredients:

- 1 zucchini, chopped
- 1 bell pepper, chopped
- 1 red onion, chopped
- 1 cup cherry tomatoes, halved
- 2 tbsp olive oil
- Salt and pepper, to taste
- Fresh parsley, chopped (optional)

Instructions:

1. Preheat the oven to 425°F (220°C).
2. Toss the zucchini, bell pepper, onion, and cherry tomatoes with olive oil, salt, and pepper.
3. Spread the veggies on a baking sheet in a single layer.
4. Roast for 20-25 minutes, stirring halfway through, until tender and slightly charred.
5. Serve warm, garnished with fresh parsley.

Grilled Chicken Salad

Ingredients:

- 2 chicken breasts
- 4 cups mixed greens (e.g., spinach, arugula, romaine)
- 1/2 cucumber, sliced
- 1/2 red onion, thinly sliced
- 1/2 cup cherry tomatoes, halved
- 1/4 cup olive oil (for grilling)
- Salt and pepper, to taste
- Dressing of choice (vinaigrette, ranch, etc.)

Instructions:

1. Preheat the grill to medium-high heat.
2. Season the chicken breasts with salt, pepper, and a drizzle of olive oil.
3. Grill the chicken for 6-7 minutes per side or until fully cooked and internal temperature reaches 165°F (75°C).
4. Slice the chicken thinly and arrange it on top of the mixed greens, cucumber, onion, and tomatoes.
5. Drizzle with your favorite dressing and serve immediately.

Pasta with Marinara Sauce

Ingredients:

- 8 oz pasta (spaghetti, penne, or your choice)
- 2 cups marinara sauce
- 1 tbsp olive oil
- 2 cloves garlic, minced
- 1/2 cup grated Parmesan cheese (optional)
- Fresh basil, chopped (optional)

Instructions:

1. Cook the pasta according to package instructions.
2. While the pasta cooks, heat olive oil in a pan over medium heat. Add garlic and cook until fragrant.
3. Stir in the marinara sauce and let it simmer for 5-7 minutes.
4. Drain the pasta and toss it with the marinara sauce.
5. Top with Parmesan cheese and fresh basil if desired.
6. Serve immediately.

Quick Stir-Fry Noodles

Ingredients:

- 8 oz noodles (egg noodles, rice noodles, or your choice)
- 2 tbsp vegetable oil
- 2 cloves garlic, minced
- 1 cup mixed veggies (bell peppers, carrots, broccoli, etc.)
- 2 tbsp soy sauce
- 1 tbsp sesame oil
- 1 tsp chili paste (optional)

Instructions:

1. Cook the noodles according to package instructions.
2. In a large skillet or wok, heat vegetable oil over medium-high heat.
3. Add garlic and veggies and stir-fry for 3-4 minutes until tender-crisp.
4. Add cooked noodles, soy sauce, sesame oil, and chili paste (if using).
5. Stir everything together and cook for an additional 2-3 minutes.
6. Serve immediately.

Shrimp Tacos

Ingredients:

- 1 lb shrimp, peeled and deveined
- 1 tbsp olive oil
- 1 tbsp taco seasoning
- 8 small tortillas
- 1 cup shredded lettuce
- 1/2 cup diced tomatoes
- 1/4 cup cilantro, chopped
- 1 lime, cut into wedges

Instructions:

1. Heat olive oil in a pan over medium-high heat.
2. Toss the shrimp in taco seasoning and cook for 2-3 minutes per side until pink and cooked through.
3. Warm the tortillas in a pan or microwave.
4. Assemble the tacos by filling each tortilla with shrimp, lettuce, tomatoes, and cilantro.
5. Squeeze fresh lime juice over the tacos before serving.

Chicken and Veggie Skewers

Ingredients:

- 2 chicken breasts, cut into cubes
- 1 bell pepper, chopped
- 1 zucchini, sliced
- 1 red onion, chopped
- 2 tbsp olive oil
- 1 tsp paprika
- Salt and pepper, to taste

Instructions:

1. Preheat the grill to medium-high heat.
2. Thread the chicken, bell pepper, zucchini, and onion onto skewers.
3. Brush with olive oil and season with paprika, salt, and pepper.
4. Grill the skewers for 8-10 minutes, turning occasionally, until the chicken is fully cooked.
5. Serve immediately.

Miso Soup

Ingredients:

- 4 cups vegetable or chicken broth
- 1/4 cup miso paste (white or red)
- 1/2 cup tofu, cubed
- 1/4 cup green onions, chopped
- 1/4 cup seaweed (wakame), rehydrated
- Soy sauce, to taste (optional)

Instructions:

1. In a pot, bring the broth to a simmer over medium heat.
2. Whisk in the miso paste until dissolved.
3. Add tofu, green onions, and seaweed to the soup and cook for 2-3 minutes.
4. Taste and adjust with soy sauce if needed.
5. Serve hot.

Veggie Soup

Ingredients:

- 1 tbsp olive oil
- 1 onion, diced
- 2 carrots, peeled and chopped
- 2 celery stalks, chopped
- 2 cups vegetable broth
- 2 cups diced tomatoes (canned or fresh)
- 1 zucchini, chopped
- 1 cup green beans, chopped
- 1 tsp dried thyme
- Salt and pepper, to taste

Instructions:

1. Heat olive oil in a large pot over medium heat.
2. Add onion, carrots, and celery, and cook for 5-7 minutes until softened.
3. Add broth, tomatoes, zucchini, green beans, thyme, salt, and pepper.
4. Bring to a simmer and cook for 20-25 minutes, or until the vegetables are tender.
5. Serve hot.

Rice Paper Rolls

Ingredients:

- 8 rice paper sheets
- 1/2 cup cooked shrimp or chicken (optional)
- 1 cup lettuce or spinach, shredded
- 1/2 cup carrots, julienned
- 1/2 cucumber, julienned
- Fresh herbs (mint, cilantro, or basil)
- Rice noodles (optional)
- Dipping sauce (peanut sauce, hoisin, or soy sauce)

Instructions:

1. Dip the rice paper in warm water for about 10-15 seconds until soft and pliable.
2. Lay the rice paper flat on a clean surface.
3. Add a small handful of lettuce, carrots, cucumber, shrimp (or chicken), and herbs.
4. Roll tightly, folding in the sides as you go.
5. Repeat with the remaining ingredients.
6. Serve with your choice of dipping sauce.

Scrambled Eggs with Spinach

Ingredients:

- 4 large eggs
- 1/2 cup fresh spinach, chopped
- 1 tbsp butter or olive oil
- Salt and pepper, to taste

Instructions:

1. Heat the butter or olive oil in a pan over medium heat.
2. Add the spinach and sauté until wilted, about 1-2 minutes.
3. Whisk the eggs in a bowl, then pour into the pan with spinach.
4. Cook, stirring frequently, until the eggs are scrambled and cooked through.
5. Season with salt and pepper to taste, then serve.

Breakfast Burrito

Ingredients:

- 2 large eggs
- 1/4 cup shredded cheese
- 1/4 cup salsa
- 1/4 cup cooked bacon or sausage (optional)
- 1 large flour tortilla
- 1/4 cup avocado, sliced
- Salt and pepper, to taste

Instructions:

1. Scramble the eggs in a bowl, season with salt and pepper.
2. Heat a pan over medium heat and scramble the eggs until cooked.
3. Warm the tortilla in a separate pan or microwave.
4. Add the scrambled eggs, cheese, salsa, avocado, and bacon or sausage (if using) to the center of the tortilla.
5. Roll up the tortilla tightly, folding in the sides.
6. Serve hot.

BLT Sandwich

Ingredients:

- 2 slices of bread, toasted
- 4 slices of cooked bacon
- 1/2 tomato, sliced
- 1-2 leaves of lettuce
- Mayonnaise or your choice of spread

Instructions:

1. Spread mayonnaise on both slices of toasted bread.
2. Layer bacon, tomato slices, and lettuce on one slice of bread.
3. Top with the second slice of bread.
4. Serve immediately.

Quick Baked Chicken Breasts

Ingredients:

- 2 boneless, skinless chicken breasts
- 1 tbsp olive oil
- 1 tsp garlic powder
- 1 tsp paprika
- Salt and pepper, to taste
- 1/2 lemon, sliced (optional)

Instructions:

1. Preheat the oven to 400°F (200°C).
2. Rub the chicken breasts with olive oil and season with garlic powder, paprika, salt, and pepper.
3. Place the chicken breasts on a baking sheet and top with lemon slices (optional).
4. Bake for 20-25 minutes, or until the internal temperature reaches 165°F (75°C).
5. Serve immediately.

Veggie Tacos

Ingredients:

- 8 small corn or flour tortillas
- 1 cup black beans, drained and rinsed
- 1 cup corn kernels (fresh or frozen)
- 1/2 cup diced tomatoes
- 1/4 cup diced red onion
- 1/4 cup fresh cilantro, chopped
- 1/2 avocado, sliced
- Lime wedges
- Salsa (optional)

Instructions:

1. Heat the tortillas in a pan over medium heat or in the microwave.
2. In a bowl, combine black beans, corn, tomatoes, red onion, and cilantro.
3. Spoon the mixture onto each tortilla.
4. Top with avocado slices, a squeeze of lime, and salsa (optional).
5. Serve immediately.

Tomato Soup with Grilled Cheese

Ingredients:

- 2 cups canned or fresh tomato puree
- 1 tbsp olive oil
- 1 onion, chopped
- 1 garlic clove, minced
- 1 cup vegetable or chicken broth
- 1/2 tsp dried basil
- Salt and pepper, to taste
- 2 slices of bread
- 2 slices of cheese (cheddar or your choice)
- Butter for grilling

Instructions:

1. In a pot, heat olive oil over medium heat and sauté the onion and garlic until soft.
2. Add the tomato puree, broth, basil, salt, and pepper. Simmer for 15 minutes.
3. Meanwhile, butter one side of each slice of bread. Place cheese between the slices and grill in a pan until golden and cheese is melted.
4. Serve the tomato soup hot with grilled cheese on the side.

Chicken Fajitas

Ingredients:

- 2 chicken breasts, thinly sliced
- 1 onion, sliced
- 1 bell pepper, sliced
- 1 tbsp olive oil
- 1 tsp cumin
- 1 tsp chili powder
- 1/2 tsp garlic powder
- 1/2 tsp paprika
- Salt and pepper, to taste
- 4 flour tortillas
- Optional toppings: sour cream, salsa, guacamole, cilantro

Instructions:

1. In a large pan, heat olive oil over medium heat.
2. Add sliced chicken and season with cumin, chili powder, garlic powder, paprika, salt, and pepper. Cook for 5-7 minutes until chicken is cooked through.
3. Add sliced onion and bell pepper to the pan and cook for another 2-3 minutes until softened.
4. Warm the tortillas in a separate pan or microwave.
5. Serve the chicken and veggie mixture in tortillas, topped with optional toppings.

Pasta Primavera

Ingredients:

- 8 oz pasta (spaghetti, penne, or your choice)
- 1 tbsp olive oil
- 1 zucchini, sliced
- 1 bell pepper, sliced
- 1 cup cherry tomatoes, halved
- 1/2 cup fresh basil, chopped
- 1/4 cup Parmesan cheese, grated
- Salt and pepper, to taste

Instructions:

1. Cook the pasta according to package instructions. Drain and set aside.
2. In a large pan, heat olive oil over medium heat.
3. Add zucchini, bell pepper, and cherry tomatoes, and cook for 5-7 minutes until softened.
4. Toss the cooked pasta with the veggies, fresh basil, and Parmesan cheese.
5. Season with salt and pepper and serve immediately.

Instant Pot Risotto

Ingredients:

- 1 tbsp olive oil
- 1 onion, chopped
- 1 cup Arborio rice
- 1/2 cup white wine (optional)
- 3 cups chicken or vegetable broth
- 1/2 cup Parmesan cheese, grated
- Salt and pepper, to taste

Instructions:

1. Turn the Instant Pot to the sauté function and heat olive oil.
2. Add onion and cook for 2-3 minutes until softened.
3. Add Arborio rice and stir for 1-2 minutes to lightly toast the rice.
4. Pour in the white wine (if using) and let it cook for a minute.
5. Add the broth, salt, and pepper, then close the lid and set to high pressure for 6 minutes.
6. Once the cooking time is up, carefully release the pressure.
7. Stir in Parmesan cheese and serve.

Burrito Bowl

Ingredients:

- 1 cup cooked rice (brown or white)
- 1 cup black beans, drained and rinsed
- 1 cup grilled chicken or beef, diced
- 1/2 cup corn kernels
- 1/4 cup salsa
- 1/4 cup guacamole
- 1/4 cup shredded cheese
- Lime wedges
- Fresh cilantro, chopped

Instructions:

1. In a bowl, layer cooked rice, black beans, corn, and grilled chicken or beef.
2. Top with salsa, guacamole, shredded cheese, and fresh cilantro.
3. Serve with lime wedges on the side for squeezing.

Quick Fried Egg Sandwich

Ingredients:

- 2 slices of bread
- 1 egg
- 1 tbsp butter
- 1 slice cheese (optional)
- Salt and pepper, to taste

Instructions:

1. Heat a pan over medium heat and melt the butter.
2. Crack the egg into the pan and cook to your desired doneness (fried or scrambled).
3. Toast the bread slices in a toaster or on a separate pan.
4. Place the fried egg on one slice of toast, add cheese if desired, and top with the second slice.
5. Serve immediately.

Ramen with Vegetables

Ingredients:

- 1 package instant ramen noodles
- 2 cups water
- 1/2 cup broccoli florets
- 1/2 cup carrots, sliced
- 1/4 cup green onions, chopped
- Soy sauce, to taste
- Sesame oil, a few drops (optional)

Instructions:

1. Bring 2 cups of water to a boil in a pot.
2. Add the instant ramen noodles and cook according to package instructions.
3. In the last 2 minutes of cooking, add the broccoli, carrots, and green onions to the pot.
4. Stir in soy sauce and sesame oil (if using).
5. Serve hot.

Chicken Pita Wraps

Ingredients:

- 2 chicken breasts, cooked and sliced
- 4 pita bread pockets
- 1/2 cup lettuce, shredded
- 1/4 cup cucumber, sliced
- 1/4 cup tomato, diced
- 2 tbsp tzatziki sauce

Instructions:

1. Warm the pita pockets in a pan or microwave.
2. Stuff each pita with sliced chicken, lettuce, cucumber, tomato, and a dollop of tzatziki sauce.
3. Serve immediately.

Sautéed Shrimp with Garlic

Ingredients:

- 1 lb shrimp, peeled and deveined
- 2 tbsp olive oil
- 4 garlic cloves, minced
- 1/4 cup fresh parsley, chopped
- Salt and pepper, to taste
- Lemon wedges

Instructions:

1. Heat olive oil in a pan over medium heat.
2. Add garlic and cook for 1 minute until fragrant.
3. Add shrimp to the pan and sauté for 3-4 minutes until pink and cooked through.
4. Season with salt, pepper, and fresh parsley.
5. Serve with lemon wedges.

Stir-Fry Tofu

Ingredients:

- 1 block firm tofu, pressed and cubed
- 2 tbsp olive oil
- 1 bell pepper, sliced
- 1 zucchini, sliced
- 1 carrot, julienned
- 2 tbsp soy sauce
- 1 tsp sesame oil (optional)

Instructions:

1. Heat olive oil in a pan over medium heat.
2. Add tofu cubes and sauté for 5-7 minutes until crispy on all sides.
3. Add bell pepper, zucchini, and carrot, and cook for another 3-4 minutes until tender.
4. Stir in soy sauce and sesame oil (if using).
5. Serve hot.

Nachos

Ingredients:

- 1 bag tortilla chips
- 1 cup shredded cheddar cheese (or your choice)
- 1/2 cup refried beans (optional)
- 1/2 cup diced tomatoes
- 1/4 cup sliced jalapeños
- 1/4 cup chopped onions
- 1/4 cup sour cream
- 1/4 cup salsa
- Guacamole (optional)

Instructions:

1. Preheat the oven to 375°F (190°C).
2. Spread tortilla chips in a single layer on a baking sheet.
3. Sprinkle the shredded cheese over the chips, then add refried beans (if using), diced tomatoes, jalapeños, and onions.
4. Bake in the oven for 10-12 minutes, or until the cheese is melted and bubbly.
5. Remove from the oven and top with sour cream, salsa, and guacamole (if desired).
6. Serve immediately.

Pita Pizza

Ingredients:

- 2 whole wheat pita breads
- 1/2 cup pizza sauce or marinara sauce
- 1 cup shredded mozzarella cheese
- Toppings of choice (pepperoni, mushrooms, onions, bell peppers, olives, etc.)
- Fresh basil (optional)

Instructions:

1. Preheat the oven to 400°F (200°C).
2. Place the pita breads on a baking sheet.
3. Spread a thin layer of pizza sauce over each pita.
4. Sprinkle the shredded mozzarella cheese over the sauce.
5. Add your choice of toppings (pepperoni, vegetables, etc.).
6. Bake in the oven for 8-10 minutes or until the cheese is melted and bubbly.
7. Garnish with fresh basil (optional) and serve immediately.

Simple Sautéed Vegetables

Ingredients:

- 1 tbsp olive oil
- 1 zucchini, sliced
- 1 bell pepper, sliced
- 1 carrot, julienned
- 1 cup broccoli florets
- Salt and pepper, to taste
- 1/2 tsp garlic powder (optional)
- Fresh herbs (optional, for garnish)

Instructions:

1. Heat olive oil in a large pan over medium heat.
2. Add the zucchini, bell pepper, carrot, and broccoli to the pan.
3. Sauté the vegetables for 5-7 minutes, stirring occasionally, until tender but still crisp.
4. Season with salt, pepper, and garlic powder (if using).
5. Garnish with fresh herbs (optional) and serve immediately.

www.ingramcontent.com/pod-product-compliance
Lightning Source LLC
LaVergne TN
LVHW081318060526
838201LV00055B/2334